WHO MADE MY LUNCH?

FROM WHEAT TO BREAD

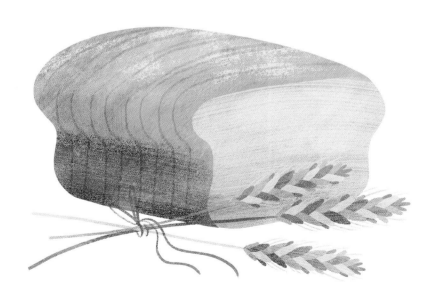

BY BRIDGET HEOS · ILLUSTRATED BY STEPHANIE FIZER COLEMAN

AMICUS ILLUSTRATED and **AMICUS INK**
are published by Amicus
P.O. Box 1329, Mankato, MN 56002
www.amicuspublishing.us

**LIBRARY OF CONGRESS
CATALOGING-IN-PUBLICATION DATA**
Names: Heos, Bridget, author. | Coleman, Stephanie Fizer, illustrator. | Heos, Bridget. Who made my lunch?
Title: From wheat to bread / by Bridget Heos ; illustrated by Stephanie Fizer Coleman.
Description: Mankato, MN : Amicus, [2018] | Series: Who made my lunch?
Identifiers: LCCN 2016054917 (print) | LCCN 2016056908 (ebook) | ISBN 9781681511184 (library binding) | ISBN 9781681512082 (e-book) | ISBN 9781681521435 (pbk.)
Subjects: LCSH: Bread—Juvenile literature. | Wheat—Juvenile literature.
Classification: LCC TX769 .H4443 2018 (print) | LCC TX769 (ebook) | DDC 641.81/5—dc23
LC record available at https://lccn.loc.gov/2016054917

EDITOR: Rebecca Glaser

DESIGNER: Kathleen Petelinsek

Printed in the United States of America
HC 10 9 8 7 6 5 4 3
PB 10 9 8 7 6 5 4 3 2 1

ABOUT THE AUTHOR
Bridget Heos is the author of more than 80 books for children. She lives in Kansas City with her husband and four children. She has passed the baking hat onto her son, but is still an avid baked goods eater.

ABOUT THE ILLUSTRATOR
Stephanie Fizer Coleman is an illustrator, tea drinker, and picky eater from West Virginia, where she lives with her husband and two silly dogs. When she's not drawing, she's getting her hands dirty in the garden or making messes in the kitchen.

Sandwiches are easy to make if you have sliced bread. But what if you had to grow the wheat and make the bread yourself? You would need to be a farmer, a miller, and a baker!

Hello, farmer! Your job is first, and you'll need a large plot of land. Look for one in the Great Plains of North America, where a lot of wheat is grown. In the fall, plant the seeds. Use a tractor to pull a machine called a drill. It drops the seeds in long rows.

The wheat sprouts quickly. But this is winter wheat. During the cold months, it goes dormant. That's sort of like taking a nap.

In spring, the wheat grows again. In summer, it turns from green to gold. Then it's time to harvest.

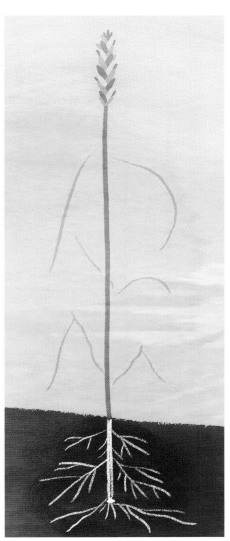

To harvest, use a combine, which does a combination of jobs.
As the farmer drives through the field, it cuts the wheat.

wheat kernels

chaff

Then the combine strips the chaff off the wheat and blows it to the ground. The part we eat, the kernel, goes into the hopper.

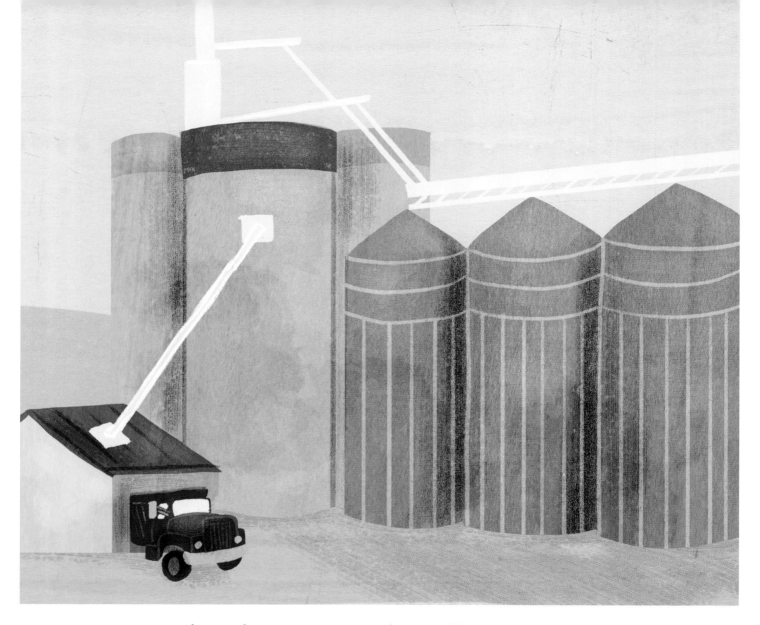

The wheat is stored in tall grain
elevators until it's ready to be milled.

Now it's your turn, miller! First, make sure the grain is healthy.

X-ray the kernels to check for insects.

Next, clean the wheat. Big machines will do the work! Screens sift out stones, hay, and more. Air blows dirt and dust away. Now the wheat is ready for grinding.

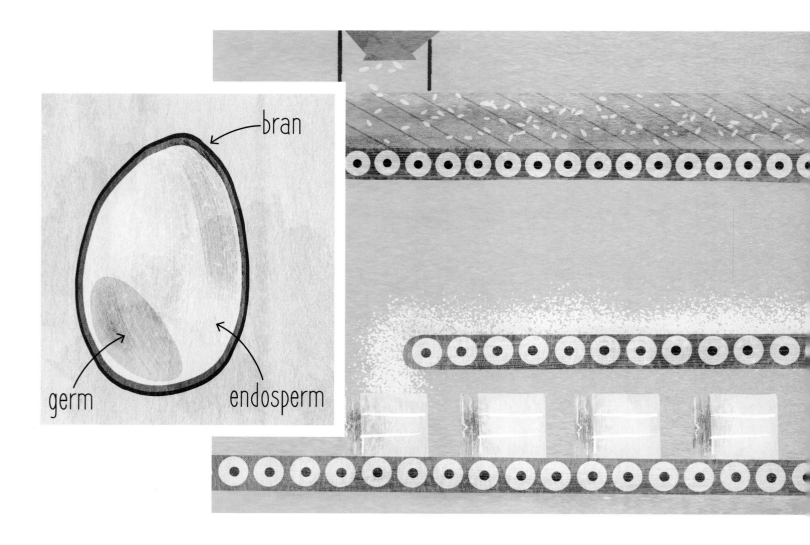

Wheat kernels have three parts. For white flour, only grind the endosperm. For whole wheat, grind the bran and germ, too. Grind and sift the wheat until you have flour.

Add vitamins and minerals to make "enriched flour." Then package the flour and ship it to factories and stores.

At the bread factory, it's dough time! The baker pours the flour, water, oil, yeast, salt, and sugar into the mixer.

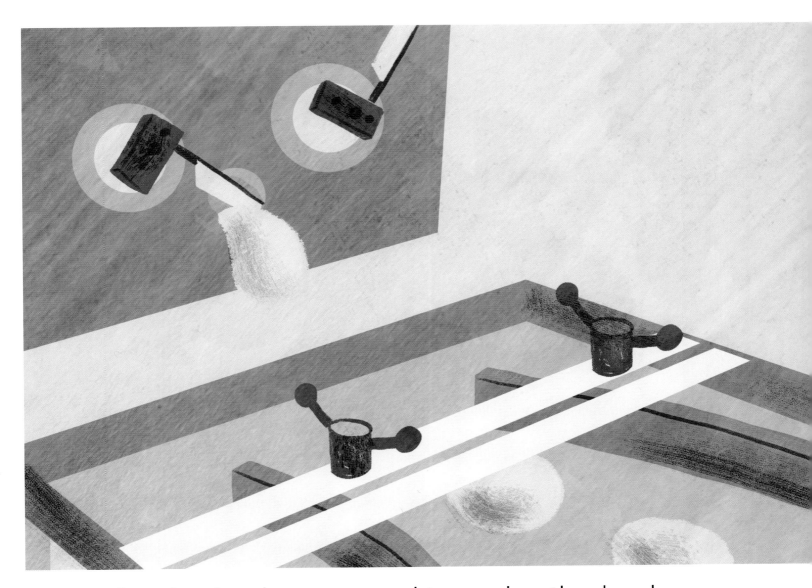

After the dough rises, a machine pushes the dough
through a tube. Knives slice off equal pieces.

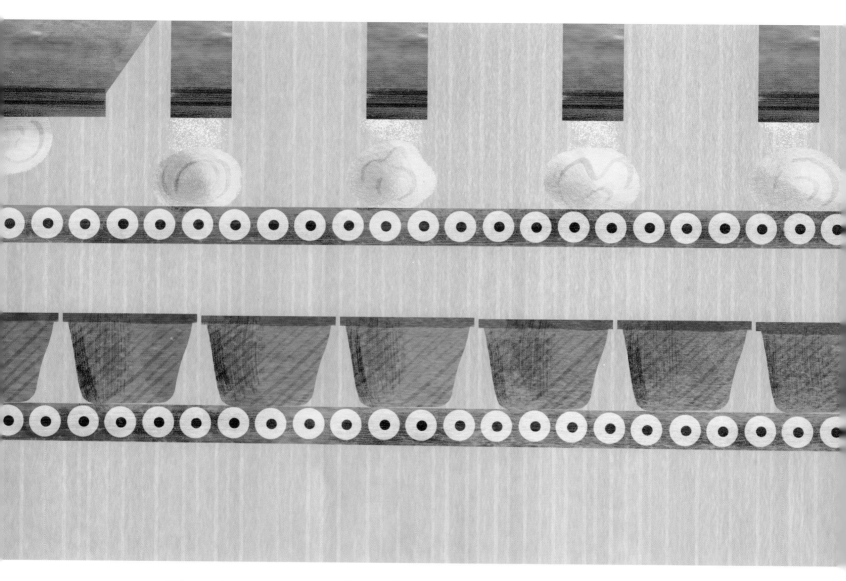

The dough is sticky. Flour sifts down to stop it
from sticking. The floury dough drops into pans.

It goes into a warm oven to rise even more.

Next, bake the dough in a hot oven.

Then let the baked loaves cool on spinning trays. Finally, the bread travels on a conveyor belt through sharp blades. And then you have it: sliced bread! The bread is packaged in bags and delivered to stores.

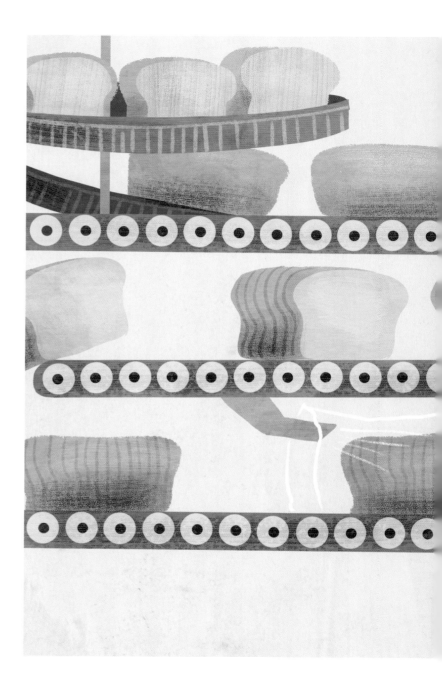

Thanks to the farmer, the miller, and the baker, you get to buy bread at the store. And now for the best job: eating the bread. Yum!

WHERE IS WHEAT GROWN?

MAP KEY
Wheat Growing Areas

GLOSSARY

chaff The outer part of a wheat plant that people can't eat.

combine A machine that harvests wheat by cutting it, separating the kernel from the chaff, and throwing away the chaff.

dormant For a plant, the state of being alive but not growing.

drill A machine that drops seeds in rows.

hopper The part of a combine where grain is stored.

kernel The part of the wheat plant that is used to make flour.

miller A person whose job is to grind grain into flour.

yeast A fungus that causes dough to rise.

WEBSITES

Bread | How It's Made | Discovery Science
http://www.sciencechannel.com/tv-shows/ how-its-made/videos/how-its-made-bread/
Watch this video to see how bread is made in a factory, thousands of loaves at a time.

Kids | Choose My Plate
http://www.choosemyplate.gov/kids
The USDA has games and activities to help you learn about food groups and how grains are part of a healthy diet.

My American Farm
http://www.myamericanfarm.org/
Games and resources from the American Farm Bureau about food and farming.

Every effort has been made to ensure that these websites are appropriate for children. However, because of the nature of the Internet, it is impossible to guarantee that these sites will remain active indefinitely or that their contents will not be altered.

READ MORE

Hayes, Amy. *Turning Wheat Into Bread*. New York: Cavendish Square Publishing, 2016.

Lassieur, Allison. *Grains*. Mankato, Minn.: Amicus, 2015.

Shaffer, Jody Jensen. *Bread*. New York: AV2 by Weigl, 2017.